Silence Behind the Blue Wall

Silence Behind the Blue Wall:
Surviving the Mental Health Stigma in Police Culture

Christopher Workman

Copyright © 2024 by Christopher Workman
All rights reserved.

No part of this publication may be reproduced, distributed, or transmitted in any form or by any means, including photocopying, recording, or other electronic or mechanical methods, without the prior written permission of the publisher, except in the case of brief quotations embodied in critical reviews and certain other noncommercial uses permitted by copyright law.

This book details the author's personal experiences with and opinions about police officer and first responder health and mental wellness. The opinions of the author, and/or any contributors is not meant to provide, legal, therapeutic, psychological, counseling or other expert advice as it relates to the subjects mentioned.

Except as specifically stated in this book, neither the author or publisher, contributors, or other representatives will be liable for damages arising out of or in connection with the use of this book. This is a comprehensive limitation of liability that applies to all damages of any kind, including (without limitation) compensatory; direct, indirect or consequential damages; loss of data, income or profit; loss of or damage to property and claims of third parties.

Please consult a trained professional before making any decisions regarding treatment about yourself or others.

IBSN: 979-8-340-70976-9 (PC), 979-8-340-72016-0 (HC)
Publisher: Independently Published (Sept. 24, 2024)
Subjects: Law Enforcement, Officer and First Responder Wellness

Dedication

To all the brave men and women in law enforcement who serve on the front lines, protecting our communities with unwavering courage. May this book provide a beacon of hope and support in your journey toward well-being and resilience.

CONTENTS

Preface ix
Introduction xi

The Thin Blue Line 3

The Rabbit Hole 15

Recognizing the Warning Signs 25

The Impact of Trauma:
Understanding the Scars that Don't Show 37

Breaking the Silence:
Building a Culture of Support 49

The Constant Battle Within 59

The Journey of Self-Care 75

A Roadmap to Resilience
Creating a Wellness Routine 93

Looking Ahead 101

Acknowledgements 107

Preface

As a police officer with a lifetime of experience in law enforcement, I have witnessed firsthand the profound impact that the demands of this profession can have on the mental health of its officers. The Blue Line is a tight-knit community, bound by a shared sense of duty and sacrifice. However, this very sense of loyalty can sometimes lead to a reluctance to acknowledge or address the invisible wounds that can accompany a career in law enforcement.

Officers in the law enforcement profession face a unique set of challenges, both on and off the job. These challenges can often take a toll on their mental health, leading to a culture of silence surrounding this important issue.

This book serves as a reminder of the importance of breaking that silence and addressing mental health within the profession. By prioritizing our well-being and building resilience, we, as well as our family, can better face the adversity that comes with the job.

If you are actively serving as officers, this book offers valuable tools and resources to help them navigate the daily challenges they face. From the stress of responding to emergencies to the emotional toll of witnessing trauma, this book provides insights on how to cope and maintain mental well-being.

If you have been in the profession for a longer period, this book acknowledges the long-term effects of stress and trauma, offering ways to address and manage these issues. For loved ones supporting law enforcement professionals, this book serves as a guide to understanding the unique challenges of the job and how to best support their loved ones.

Overall, this book serves as a testament to the importance of addressing mental health within the law enforcement profession. By providing valuable tools, resources, and insights, it aims to break the silence and prioritize the well-being of those who serve and protect our communities.

Whether you are an active officer, a veteran, or a loved one, this book is a valuable resource for building resilience and maintaining mental wellness in the face of the challenges of the job.

Introduction

The blue line is often portrayed as a symbol of strength and unwavering courage, a line that stands between chaos and order. While this image is true in many ways, it is crucial to recognize that law enforcement officers are human beings, with vulnerabilities and emotional needs like anyone else. The demands of the job, the constant exposure to violence and trauma, and the pressure to maintain a strong and stoic façade can take a toll on mental health.

This expectation can create a toxic work environment where officers feel they must suppress their emotions and avoid seeking help for their mental health struggles. This can lead to a sense of isolation and further exacerbate mental health issues. Studies have shown that police officers are at a higher risk for experiencing PTSD, depression, anxiety, occupational and burnout, moral injury, and vicarious trauma than the general population. This is not a sign of weakness, but rather a reflection of the inherent challenges of the job.

As a result, there has been a growing awareness and recognition of the prevalence of mental health issues within the law enforcement community. Efforts are being made to provide support and resources for officers to address their mental health needs and break the stigma surrounding seeking help. This is an important step in promoting the overall well-being of law enforcement officers and ensuring they have the necessary support to continue serving their communities.

This book guides law enforcement officers to navigate the emotional demands of their profession and build resilience in the face of adversity. Drawing on my own experiences as a police officer and in dealing with my mental health, I will provide practical tools, techniques, and insights that can help you prioritize your well-being and create a more balanced and fulfilling life. It's time to break the silence and embrace the importance of mental health in our profession. Together, we can build a culture of support and understanding that allows law enforcement officers to thrive on and off duty.

When we can express our recovery openly, we have the potential to assist those who are suffering in silence. This will lead to a sense of vicarious resilience.

"The end of all knowledge should be service to others."

– Cesar Chavez

The Thin Blue Line

The blue line. It's a symbol of strength, of unwavering dedication, of courage in the face of danger. We wear it proudly, as a badge of honor and a testament to our commitment to protecting and serving. But what happens when the line that protects us begins to crack under the weight of the unseen burdens we carry?

The life of a law enforcement officer isn't for the faint of heart. We face situations that most people could never imagine, and witness horrors that haunt us long after the sirens have faded. We're expected to be strong, unflinching, and the ones who bring calm to chaos. But somewhere along the line, the weight of it all can become too heavy, the pressure too immense. The blue line, once a source of pride, starts to feel like a weight around our necks.

I know this firsthand. I spent years on the force, a young officer, eager to make a difference. I saw my fair share of violence, faced down criminals, and felt the rush of adrenaline that came with every close call. But I also have carried the burden of those experiences through many years, the memory of the fear in the eyes of victims, and the echo of the screams that still echoed in my ears long after the scene had been cleared.

The world expects law enforcement officers to be impervious to the darkness we encounter, to walk through fire and emerge unscathed. But that's simply not the reality. We are human beings, with emotions and vulnerabilities just like everyone else. We experience stress, anxiety, depression, and trauma just as deeply, if not more so, than the general population. The badge I wore, began to feel like a reminder of my struggles rather than my honor. I knew I wasn't alone in this; many of my colleagues had their demons to battle. We put on a brave face, but the weight of our service was taking its toll. It was as if the line that once protected us now held us captive, a silent prisoner of the job.

The public saw our uniform and expected invincibility, but beneath the surface, we were fighting our own battles, wishing for an understanding that often felt out of reach. The job had changed me, and I knew it. I could feel the shift in my perspective, a subtle but persistent change in how I viewed the world. I became more cautious, more aware of the potential dangers lurking in every shadow. Every call felt like a potential powder keg, and I found myself bracing for the worst-case scenario.

I knew that this heightened sense of awareness was a survival mechanism, but it also took a toll on my mental health. It was a constant internal struggle, this battle between our chosen duty and the human cost it exacted. We needed an outlet, a way to release the pressure without breaking the blue line. It was a delicate balance and one that we often struggled to maintain. Yet, despite the challenges, we persevered. We found strength in our shared experiences and supported each other through the darkest of times. It was this unspoken bond that kept us going, a silent promise to never let the line break, no matter the burden.

We often struggled to maintain an image of strength in law enforcement. The pressure to appear invincible was immense, but we knew deep down that we were not. The weight of our experiences and the toll it took on our mental health was something we couldn't ignore. Despite the challenges and societal expectations, we persevered. The bond we shared as officers kept us going, a silent promise to never let one another fall. We knew that we could rely on each other during the darkest of times, and that gave us the strength to continue. But the silence surrounding mental health in law enforcement made our struggles even more profound. We were expected to hide our wounds and carry on as if nothing was wrong. This pressure to maintain an image of invincibility only added to the weight on our shoulders. It was a constant battle between the expectations of society and the reality of our struggles.

This book is about acknowledging those wounds, understanding the unique challenges we face, and building resilience, not just for our careers, but for our lives. It's about learning how to navigate the emotional demands of our profession, find tools for self-care, and build a support system that can help us cope with the inevitable darkness we encounter.

It's about reclaiming our strength, not just as officers, but as human beings. It's about realizing that seeking help is not a sign of weakness, but a sign of courage, a sign that we are willing to fight for our mental well-being, just as fiercely as we fight for the safety of our communities.

I'll be sharing personal anecdotes, real-life experiences, and practical techniques that have helped me, and countless others, navigate the difficult realities of law enforcement. We will be diving into the importance of self-awareness, the power of mindfulness, and the significance of building healthy relationships.

As we embark on this journey towards building healthy relationships, it's important to remember that this book is not a quick fix. It is not a cure-all solution to our struggles, but rather a starting point. It serves as a guide, a roadmap to navigate the silent war within ourselves. It empowers us to acknowledge our invisible wounds and take the necessary steps toward healing and resilience.

But this book is more than just a guide, it is a *call to action*. It urges us to break the silence that often surrounds mental health and well-being. It encourages us to have open and honest conversations about our struggles and to seek support from those around us. By embracing resilience as a proactive approach to our mental well-being, we can create a safe and supportive environment for ourselves and those around us. So, let's not delay any further.

Let's begin this journey towards building healthy relationships and nurturing our mental well-being. Let's embrace resilience and break the silence, as we take the necessary steps towards healing and growth. This book may not have all the answers, but it is a powerful tool that will guide us on this journey and help us build a stronger, more resilient version of ourselves.

Invisible Wounds

I remember the first time I saw a dead body, the scene that unfolded before me that night shattered my innocence. The victim, a young woman, lay lifeless on the living room floor, her eyes staring blankly at the ceiling. The air was heavy with the metallic scent of blood, and the silence was deafening, broken only by the distant sirens of the arriving units.

As I stood there, surrounded by the shattered remnants of a life, I couldn't help but think about the countless other tragic events that I had witnessed throughout my career. Each one brings with it a new wave of emotions and a deeper understanding of the fragility of life.

It was a constant reminder of just how quickly everything can change and how little control we truly have. The knot in my stomach only grew tighter as I reflected on the countless lives that had been lost and the ripple effect it had on their loved ones. Despite the years of experience, each encounter left its unique mark. Some were more gruesome than others, but they all whispered in the shadows of my mind, haunting me long after the scene had been cleared. I couldn't help but wonder how many more shattered lives I would have to witness before I became numb to it all. It was a thought that filled me with sadness and a sense of resignation, knowing that this was the reality of the world we live in. But amidst all the pain and suffering, there were also moments of hope and resilience.

This was when I first discovered the idea of vicarious resilience. Experiencing the struggles and challenges faced by others really opened my eyes to this concept. It's fascinating how we can feel a sense of strength and hope just by observing how people navigate their own hardships. When we see someone overcoming adversity, it not only impacts them but also resonates with us, creating a shared experience that can inspire and uplift.

Witnessing the strength of the human spirit come into focus, as I saw people rise above their tragedies and carry on with their lives. This gave me a sliver of hope, a reminder that despite the fragility of life, we are all capable of great courage and resilience. That if they, in the face of great tragedy and adversity were able to move forward and carry on, then I also had the capacity to do the same, and as I walked away from another shattered life, I held onto that glimmer of hope, knowing that it was what kept me going in this often harsh and unforgiving world.

There are traffic accidents, the violent crimes, the suicides, the endless cycle of pain and suffering that we are exposed to daily. Every encounter leaving its mark, etching itself into our memories, whispering in the shadows of our minds. And as the years passed, those memories began to weigh me down. I found myself growing increasingly irritable, easily startled, haunted by recurring nightmares. The line between work and life became blurred, and I started to feel like I was constantly on edge, like I was carrying the weight of the world on my shoulders.

I wasn't alone. I saw it in the eyes of my colleagues, the way they flinched at sudden noises, the haunted look in their eyes when they were off duty. We all carried our invisible wounds, scars that weren't visible to the naked eye but that etched themselves deeply into our souls.

We were expected to be strong, to be pillars of calm amid chaos, but we were crumbling from within. We were fighting a silent war, a battle against the unseen demons that haunted our minds and threatened to consume us.

Nowhere to Go

There were many times I had felt the despair and dread of those many incidents had been imprinted deep in my mind. But I remember one night, after a particularly harrowing shift, sitting at the kitchen table, staring blankly at the remains of a meal I barely touched. I felt like I was slowly losing myself, drowning in the pressures and expectations of my job. I was a shell of the person I used to be, and I didn't know how to break free from the cycle. My wife was talking to me and I was not hearing a word of what she was saying, it was a distant whisper that was not breaking through my current diffusion from reality.

I needed help, but the stigma surrounding mental health in law enforcement made it impossible for me to reach out. I was constantly surrounded by strong, stoic individuals who prided themselves on their toughness and resilience. As a result, I was trapped in a cycle of silence, afraid of being seen as weak, of being judged, of jeopardizing my career. I couldn't risk asking for help and admitting that I was struggling because it would go against the unspoken code of strength that was ingrained in our profession.

I was left to suffer in silence, feeling like I was the only one struggling with my mental health. I didn't realize that many of my colleagues were also facing similar challenges, but we were all too afraid to speak up. The fear of being seen as weak and the potential consequences on our careers kept us trapped in our battles. It wasn't until I hit rock bottom that I realized I needed to break the silence and seek help. It was a dark time, a time of isolation and despair. I felt like I was drowning, and there was no one around to throw me a lifeline. But then I stumbled upon a resource that would change my life.

It was a peer support group, a safe space for officers to talk about their experiences, their struggles, and their fears, without judgment. It was a haven in the storm, a place where I could finally let down my guard, share my burdens, and know that I wasn't alone.

My struggles as a police officer had taken a toll on my mental and emotional well-being. For years, I had been shouldering the weight of my burdens, believing that it was a sign of weakness to seek help. But in a moment of desperation, I finally let down my guard and reached out for support. It was the best decision I ever made.

Through the support group, I discovered a network of other officers who had been through similar struggles. They understood the challenges and pressures of the job, and I no longer felt alone. I learned that it was okay to not be okay, that it was okay to acknowledge the wounds I carried, to seek help, and to fight for my well-being. I found comfort in knowing that I was not weak for needing help, but rather, it was a sign of strength to recognize and address my struggles. As I continued to attend the support group meetings, I began to open up and share my experiences with others. It was a cathartic experience to be able to talk about my struggles without fear of judgment. I realized that I was not alone in my journey and that there was a community of officers who were there to support each other through difficult times. And in that journey of healing, I realized that resilience wasn't just about surviving, it was about thriving. I also realized that I was experiencing posttraumatic growth. Where resilience is about bouncing back, posttraumatic growth is about bouncing forward and, about building a life that it was filled with purpose and meaning, even amidst the challenges we face.

Looking back, I can confidently say that this decision was transformative. It allowed me to connect with others who understood my struggles and provided me with the tools to navigate my challenges more effectively. Embracing vulnerability and seeking help turned out to be the most empowering choice I could have made, leading me toward a path of recovery and renewed strength.

But there was another challenge I was facing; one I'd kept secret even from the support group. A challenge I felt too ashamed to admit even to myself. As I sat in the dimly lit room, listening to others share their stories of trauma and loss, I knew I had to face it head-on.

The Rabbit Hole

Later that day, as I was home just pondering the things that I had been dreading and the anxiety that was overwhelming me.

I walked outside and found myself alone, in my driveway, just waking in circles, my mind was in a million places and I had an overwhelming feeling of dread and despair. I was scared and did not know what was happening to me, my heart pounding out of my chest, sweating, my body trembling,

My mind wondering if I should just…

There was a battle going on inside of my head, one that had never been there before. Through all of the things that I had encountered in my personal and professional life over the years, I would have never thought of just making this feeling go away.

What am I going to do?

But that was not the answer, my hands were shaking as I reached for the phone. My voice was barely a whisper as I dialed the number.

"Hello?"

The voice on the other end was calm, reassuring. "This is the confidential hotline for law enforcement officers."

"I need help." My voice cracked. "I need help."

I took a deep breath, and for the first time in years, I allowed myself to speak the truth, to confess the darkness that had been consuming me.

"I think I'm... I think I'm losing control."

The silence on the other end felt heavy, suffocating.

It seemed to go on forever, though it was only seconds.

Then, a voice, soft but firm, spoke into my ear. "It's okay. You're not alone. We can help. But first, I need you to answer a few questions. Have you... have you ever thought about hurting yourself?"

I was silent, I could hear my heart pounding, the hairs on my arms standing on end, my mouth was dry as I answered in a soft calm voice

"Yes, I have."

I had never fully planned my escape from this turmoil, but I have had those feelings pop into my head when the day was the darkest and it was becoming more and more prevalent. But today, I scared myself, the thought a feeling had crossed my mind that I thought would never be, if I had the access to a gun at this moment, what would it be like to just put it to my head and it all go away?

This was the first moment I voiced these feelings to someone else. The thoughts had been swirling in my mind, a tempest of emotions and reflections that seemed to gain momentum whenever the chaos of daily life subsided. It was as if the noise around me would drown out my inner turmoil, but in those rare moments of stillness, clarity would wash over me like a gentle tide, bringing with it a flood of realizations I could no longer ignore.

The weight of my unspoken thoughts pressing down on me, a burden I had carried alone for far too long. Each time I tried to articulate them, the words would slip away, elusive and intangible, like wisps of smoke. But now, as I heard a calm, soothing voice over the phone, from someone who seemed to genuinely care, the dam broke. I took a deep breath, feeling the air fill my lungs, and finally allowed the words to spill forth.

It reminded me of Alice's journey down the rabbit hole into Wonderland, a descent into the unknown where everything was both familiar and utterly strange. Just as Alice encountered peculiar characters and bewildering landscapes.

As I spoke, I could see feel a sense of recognition from the voice on the line, an acknowledgment that perhaps they too had wandered through their own Wonderland of emotions. It was a moment of connection, a bridge built between my inner chaos and the outside world. I realized that voicing my feelings was not just an act of vulnerability; it was an invitation to explore the depths of my own heart and mind, to confront the shadows that had lingered there for too long.

In that moment, I understood that sharing my thoughts was the first step toward unraveling the tangled threads of my experience. Just as Alice learned to navigate the absurdities of her surroundings, I too was beginning to find my way through the labyrinth of my emotions, one word at a time.

My deep loneliness and fear began to transform, and I started to consider that there might be a way to break free from this suffering. It felt as though a ray of light had cut through the thick fog of despair that had surrounded me for so long. and with that change came a flicker of hope. I recognized that the journey ahead would not be easy; it would likely be filled with challenges and hurdles that would test my determination. Yet, for the first time in ages, I felt a spark of resolve igniting within me.

This journey would require more than just a moment of inspiration; it would call for commitment and dedication every day. It also meant embracing discomfort and uncertainty, pushing myself beyond the safe boundaries of my comfort zone. It would require me to take whatever steps necessary to achieve my goal — whether it was reaching out to a friend, seeking professional support, or simply allowing myself to feel and process my emotions instead of burying them deep within.

> *"I can't go back to yesterday – because I was a different person then."* –Lewis Carroll, Alice in Wonderland

Clean Out Your Mental Closet

There was only one way begin to heal and change the narrative, it was time to clean out my mental closet, confronting all the skeletons I've worked so hard to keep concealed. It would mean sifting through the clutter of my thoughts and emotions, unearthing may years of memories and visions of pain and sorrow that I've buried deep beneath layers of denial and distraction.

With each revelation, I would have to confront the emotions tied to these memories—anger, sadness, and perhaps even shame. It would be a process of reckoning, where I would need to acknowledge the impact that all of my personal and professional experiences have had on my life and the choices I have made along the way. I would have to allow myself to feel the pain, to sit with it, rather than pushing it aside as I've done for so long.

This journey of cleaning out my mental closet would not only be about facing the past but also about understanding how it has shaped me. I would need to reflect on the lessons learned, the resilience built, and the strength gained from overcoming adversity. It would be an opportunity for growth, a chance to transform those skeletons from sources of shame into stepping stones toward healing and self-acceptance.

In confronting each skeleton, I would be reclaiming my narrative, taking ownership of my story. I would learn to embrace the imperfections and complexities of my life, recognizing that they are all part of what makes me human. In this process, I would find clarity and freedom, allowing me to move forward with a renewed sense of purpose and authenticity.

Cleaning out the mental closet will be a challenging but necessary step toward living a more honest and fulfilling life. We can replace limiting beliefs with empowering ones, allowing us to pursue our passions and dreams with renewed vigor. If we can shed the weight of past disappointments and negative self-talk, we open ourselves up to new opportunities and experiences that align with our authentic selves.

This is not a one-shot deal, a one-time event, cleaning out the mental closet is an ongoing journey. It requires regular reflection and a commitment to self-improvement. When we continually assess our thoughts and emotions, we can have the ability to have a clear and open mental space that allows us to live authentically and fully. In doing so, we pave the way for a more satisfying and meaningful life, one that is true to who we are at our core.

It was with this new found perspective, I finally began to envision a future where I could reclaim my joy and sense of self, imagined the possibility of forming deeper connections with others, find comfort in shared experiences, and rediscover passions that had long been overshadowed by my pain. It was time to clean out my mental closet and allow healing to begin.

This was it, this was the time, time to make that call and I reached out to a professional therapist and began to surround myself with supportive friends who understood my struggles, because they had or were there themselves.

"If you want to improve your life immediately, clean out a closet. Often, it's what we hold onto that holds us back." – Cheryl Richardson

Recognizing The Warning Signs

The thin blue line is a powerful symbol. It represents the bond of brotherhood and the unwavering commitment to protecting our communities. But behind that line, there's another struggle, a silent war that can wear down even the toughest officers. We talked about the invisible wounds of law enforcement in the last chapter. Now, it's time to look at those wounds more closely – to understand how they manifest and to learn how to spot the warning signs before they become overwhelming.

Imagine you're walking down a quiet street, just another night on patrol. A call comes in, a domestic disturbance. You arrive, sirens blaring, lights flashing, and find a tense scene. Angry voices, a broken vase, maybe a fear-stricken child clinging to their mother. You're trained to de-escalate, to mediate, to restore peace. The tension is so thick in the air that it almost feels palpable. It's as if you could reach out and touch it, grasp it in your hands. But instead, you stand there, rooted to the ground, watching as the anger and fear swirl around you. It's a familiar scene, one you've seen too many times before. Yet, somehow, this time it feels different.

As you survey the crowd, you can see the signs of unease etched on their faces. The furrowed brows, the clenched fists, the darting, suspicious glances. And you feel it too, deep in your gut. A knot forms, slowly at first, but then tightening with each passing moment. Your spine prickles with a chill as if warning you of impending danger. But it's not just a physical response, it's something deeper, something more intuitive. A sense of unease, a feeling that things are about to escalate.

> *"If you listen to your body when it whispers, you won't have to hear it scream." Adapted from Cherokee Proverb*

This feeling, this sense of unease, is often the first whisper of a larger issue. It's the body speaking a language we often neglect to listen to. It's telling us something isn't right. And in this moment, you know that you must act, to do something to diffuse the tension and restore peace. But you also know that this is not going to be easy. The stakes are high, the emotions are running strong, and you have a difficult task ahead of you.

The body, it turns out, is a remarkably accurate gauge of our mental and emotional state. It's a living, breathing alarm system, constantly monitoring our internal world and sending out signals whenever something is amiss.

These physical manifestations are not mere coincidences; they are the body's way of communicating the emotional turmoil we may be experiencing. By recognizing these signals, we can begin to understand the underlying emotions that may be influencing our physical state, allowing us to address them more effectively.

The Body Speaks: Decoding the Warning Signs

Your body has a unique way of expressing its needs and concerns, and it's crucial to tune in to those cues. This might include recognizing when you feel unusually tired, experiencing persistent aches, or noticing changes in your mood or appetite.

When you dismiss these signs, they often grow in volume and urgency, making it increasingly difficult to ignore. For example, a slight feeling of anxiety might develop into chronic stress if not acknowledged and managed. By taking the time to understand what your body is telling you, you can begin to identify the root causes of any discomfort or distress you may be experiencing.

This process of self-awareness can lead to better health choices, such as adjusting your diet, incorporating more physical activity, or seeking professional help when necessary.

Understanding these signals is crucial. It's like knowing the difference between a squeaky wheel that needs a little oil and a full-blown engine breakdown. Being able to identify the early warning signs of stress, anxiety, and burnout can make a huge difference in maintaining your mental well-being.

Think back to the domestic disturbance call. How did your body react? Did your heart race? Did you feel a surge of adrenaline? Did you feel your muscles tense up? These are classic signs of the body's "fight or flight" response, a natural survival mechanism triggered by perceived threats.

Here are some common warning signs to look out for:

Physical:
- Fatigue:
  Persistent fatigue, even after getting enough sleep,
- Muscle tension,
  Aches and pains in your neck, shoulders, or back.
- Changes in appetite:
  Overeating or undereating.
- Sleep disturbances:
  Difficulty falling asleep, staying asleep, or waking up feeling unrested.
- Headaches:
  Frequent or severe headaches.
- Stomach problems:

- Indigestion, nausea, or other digestive issues.
  - Changes in physical appearance:
  - Unintentional weight loss or gain, changes in skin or hair.
  - Increased illness:
  - Frequent colds, flu, or other infections.

Emotional:
  - Irritability:
  - Short fuse, easily frustrated or angered.
  - Anxiety:
  - Feeling restless, on edge, or worried.
  - Depression:
  - Feeling sad, hopeless, or withdrawn.
  - Lack of motivation:
  - Difficulty concentrating, feeling uninterested in things you used to enjoy.
  - Social withdrawal:
  - Pulling away from friends and family.
  - Emotional numbness:
  - Feeling detached or disconnected from your emotions.
  - Increased substance use:
  - Turning to alcohol or drugs to cope.

Ignoring these warning signs or resorting to alternative methods to manage the symptoms can plunge you deeper into a realm of uncertainty. I found myself desperately attempting to set aside these overwhelming emotions, hoping that by doing so, I could regain a sense of control over my life.

It's a common struggle, where the desire to avoid discomfort often leads us to ignore the very issues that need our attention. This avoidance can manifest in various ways—distracting ourselves with work, immersing in social activities, or even resorting to unhealthy habits.

Each time I brushed aside my feelings, I felt a fleeting sense of relief, but it was always short-lived. The underlying issues remained, festering beneath the surface, waiting for the moment when they would inevitably resurface, often with greater intensity. This cycle of denial and temporary relief creates a false sense of security, lulling us into a belief that we have everything under control, when in reality, we are merely postponing the inevitable confrontation with our emotions. I was trying everything that I could to push these feelings aside.

It would work, but just for a little while before the feelings of dread and despair would return, there is no getting away from it unless you make that decision to listen to the signs your body is giving you. It will only get louder and more prevalent unless you seek to attack the problem at its source.

Beyond the Body: Recognizing Your Triggers

While these physical and emotional signs are important clues, they're often just the tip of the iceberg.

Ultimately, this journey of self-discovery is vital for fostering a healthier relationship with yourself. It encourages you to listen to your body and respond with compassion rather than judgment. Instead of dismissing feelings of discomfort or distress as mere inconveniences, you learn to view them as valuable insights into your emotional and physical health.

As you become more attuned to your triggers and the messages they convey, you will find yourself better equipped to navigate the complexities of your emotional and physical landscape. This heightened awareness not only promotes self-acceptance but also paves the way for greater well-being and resilience. By embracing this journey, you develop a deeper sense of self-awareness and empowerment, allowing you to make informed choices that support your overall health and happiness. In doing so, you create a nurturing environment for personal growth and healing, ultimately leading to a more fulfilling and balanced life.

Specific situations, events, or even personal thoughts can act as triggers that induce feelings of stress, anxiety, or a sense of being overwhelmed. These triggers can be external, such as a challenging work environment, a looming deadline, or a difficult conversation with a loved one, or they can be internal, stemming from one's own thoughts, beliefs, or past experiences.

Here's an exercise to help you identify your triggers:

Think back to the last few weeks or months.

What situations, events, or interactions left you feeling emotionally drained, on edge, or irritable? What specific thoughts or feelings seem to lead to those reactions?
Write down your observations.

Example:
Let's say you're a patrol officer who gets into a heated argument with a suspect. You manage to de-escalate the situation, but you're left feeling shaken and on edge.

- Trigger:
  Confrontation with a combative individual.

- Physical Response:
  Racing heart, rapid breathing, muscle tension.

- Emotional Response:
    Anger, frustration, fear, anxiety.

Throughout my career I have made it a common practice to review my interactions with people, sometimes to a fault. I would think about how that call went, the things that I had said, things they had said to me. If the suspect or witness I was speaking with got agitated or combative I would replay the interaction in my head, what it was I may have done or said that triggered that reaction, and on some occasions, it was me that travelled the wrong path, or said something that sparked that confrontation.

By recognizing these triggers, individuals can take proactive measures to reduce their effects, promote a healthier emotional state, and lay the groundwork for enhancing their emotional intelligence. This process begins with self-awareness, where individuals learn to identify specific situations, thoughts, or interactions that provoke strong emotional responses. By understanding these triggers, they can develop strategies to manage their reactions more effectively.

This might involve developing coping mechanisms such as deep breathing exercises, journaling, or engaging in physical activity to release pent-up tension. We begin to see the value in seeking support from friends, family, or mental health professionals that can provide valuable insights and strategies for managing these triggers effectively.

The journey of recognizing and addressing emotional triggers is a vital step toward achieving emotional resilience. It empowers us to take control of our emotional well-being, leading to a more balanced and fulfilling life.

As we continue to grow in their emotional intelligence, we not only enhance our own lives but also positively impact those around us, fostering a more empathetic and understanding community.

The Impact of Trauma: Understanding the Scars that Don't Show

Many of us have a different view of what the word trauma means, so we cannot proceed without first defining trauma. It is not merely defined by the external situations an individual faces, such as accidents, natural disasters, violence, or loss. Instead, trauma is fundamentally rooted in the internal reactions and psychological changes that these events trigger within a person.

When someone experiences a traumatic event, their immediate responses can vary significantly, influenced by numerous factors including their personal history, coping strategies, and available support systems. These reactions can manifest in various forms, such as intense fear, helplessness, or horror, and can lead to enduring emotional and psychological effects.

"Trauma is not what happens to you, it is what happens inside of you as a result of what happens to you" - Ernest Stevens

---

As a law enforcement officer, you are often exposed to the worst of humanity. The trauma of these experiences can leave deep emotional scars that may not be readily apparent. These scars can manifest as anger, frustration, fear, and anxiety, making it difficult to cope with daily life. By understanding your triggers, you can start to develop strategies to manage your reactions to them.

Managing your reactions to trauma may involve various techniques such as deep breathing exercises, grounding exercises, or seeking support from trusted colleagues or mental health professionals. These strategies can help you to regulate your emotions and cope with the intense feelings that may arise. By recognizing and addressing the impact of trauma, you can take steps toward healing and finding peace within yourself.

It is important to remember that healing from trauma is a journey and may not be a linear process. It's essential to be patient and gentle with yourself as you work through your experiences and emotions. With the right support and coping mechanisms, you can learn to manage and overcome the scars left by trauma.

It's crucial to prioritize your mental well-being and seek help when needed. The thin blue line often means encountering situations that most people never experience. It means witnessing violence, dealing with suffering, and confronting the dark side of humanity.

And those experiences can leave scars, even if they're not visible to the naked eye.

Trauma, whether it's a single incident or prolonged exposure to violence and stress, can have a profound impact on our mental health. It can lead to a wide range of symptoms, including anxiety, depression, and post-traumatic stress disorder.

- Post-traumatic stress disorder (PTSD): This is a serious mental health condition that can occur after a traumatic event. Symptoms can include intrusive thoughts, flashbacks, nightmares, emotional numbness, avoidance, and hyperarousal.

- Anxiety: Trauma can make it difficult to feel safe and secure. You might feel constantly on edge, anticipating danger, or worrying about things that you wouldn't normally worry about.

- Depression: Trauma can lead to feelings of sadness, hopelessness, and worthlessness. You might lose interest in things you used to enjoy, have difficulty concentrating, or experience changes in your sleep or appetite.

- Burnout: Trauma and stress can take a toll on your body and mind, leading to emotional exhaustion, cynicism, and a sense of detachment from your work.

For those in law enforcement, the thin blue line not only represents a career but also a way of life. It means constantly being on guard, ready to face any situation that may arise. This constant state of alertness can take a toll on mental well-being, as officers are exposed to traumatic events regularly.

Barbara Rubel, a leading authority on compassion fatigue, secondary trauma, and vicarious trauma describes this as work-related exposure to the traumas we develop through the things that we witness daily in her book Living Blue.

Compassion fatigue, secondary trauma, and vicarious trauma are interconnected concepts that highlight the emotional toll experienced by professionals who work closely with individuals facing trauma. These terms encapsulate the psychological strain that arises from being repeatedly exposed to the distressing narratives and experiences of others, particularly in fields such as healthcare, social work, counseling, and emergency response.

Compassion fatigue refers to the gradual erosion of the ability to empathize with others due to the overwhelming nature of their suffering. It often manifests as a sense of emotional exhaustion, where caregivers find it increasingly difficult to connect with their clients or patients. This fatigue can lead to a diminished capacity for compassion, making it challenging for professionals to provide the support and care that those in need require. Over time, this can create a cycle of disengagement, where the caregiver becomes less effective in their role, further exacerbating feelings of guilt and inadequacy.

Secondary trauma, on the other hand, occurs when individuals indirectly experience the trauma of others through their work. This can happen when professionals hear detailed accounts of traumatic events or witness the aftermath of such experiences. The emotional impact can be profound, leading to symptoms similar to those of post-traumatic stress disorder (PTSD), including intrusive thoughts, heightened anxiety, and emotional distress. Professionals may find themselves reliving the trauma vicariously, which can disrupt their personal lives and relationships.

Vicarious trauma is a broader concept that encompasses the cumulative effects of exposure to trauma over time. It refers to the transformation in a professional's worldview and sense of safety as a result of their work with trauma survivors. This can lead to a pervasive sense of hopelessness, cynicism, and a distorted perception of reality. Individuals may begin to view the world as a more dangerous place, which can impact their overall mental health and well-being.

The emotional impact of these experiences can be profound, leading to feelings of helplessness, emotional numbness, and burnout. Professionals may struggle to cope with the demands of their daily tasks, feeling overwhelmed by the weight of the suffering they witness. This can result in a decline in job satisfaction, increased absenteeism, and a higher turnover rate in professions that require emotional labor.

Despite being trained to handle these situations, it is still important for officers to recognize when they need help and not be afraid to seek it. The dark side of humanity is something that most people never have to face. However, for those in law enforcement, it can be a daily reality.

Our empathetic responses to traumatic experiences are witnessing - acts of violence, dealing with the aftermath of tragedies, and confronting the worst in people, can leave a lasting impact on an officer's mental health.

These experiences can create invisible scars that may not be obvious to others but can greatly affect a person's well-being and daily life, making it difficult to function and cope with everyday challenges.

It is essential to prioritize self-care and seek support. This may include engaging in regular supervision or consultation, participating in training on trauma-informed care, and developing healthy coping strategies. Creating a supportive work environment that encourages open dialogue about these challenges can also foster resilience and promote mental well-being

Coping with Trauma: A Path to Healing

Coping with trauma is a unique journey for everyone, as no two individuals experience it in the same way.

Each individual possesses unique coping mechanisms and support systems that reflect their personal experiences, backgrounds, and emotional needs. This diversity highlights the critical importance for law enforcement officers to prioritize their mental health actively. Given the high-stress nature of their work, officers often encounter challenging situations that can take a toll on their psychological well-being.

Recognizing the signs of stress, anxiety, or burnout is essential, as is understanding that seeking help is not a sign of weakness but rather a proactive step towards maintaining mental health. Officers should feel empowered to reach out for support, whether through professional counseling, peer support programs, or community resources.

Many officers may feel pressure to maintain a tough exterior and push through traumatic experiences without seeking support. However, this can lead to long-term mental health issues and impact their overall well-being. The path to healing from trauma is not a linear one and may involve ups and downs.

When law enforcement officers can prioritize their mental health, they create a foundation for both personal well-being and professional effectiveness. The nature of their work often exposes them to high-stress situations, traumatic events, and the emotional toll of dealing with crime and suffering. By actively addressing their mental health needs, officers can develop coping strategies and resilience that enable them to navigate these challenges more effectively.

> *"It's OK not to be OK, but it is not OK to Stay that Way"* – Ernest Stevens

This commitment to mental well-being fosters a healthier work environment, where officers feel supported and empowered to seek help when needed. As a result, they are less likely to experience burnout, anxiety, or depression, which can impair their judgment and decision-making abilities. When officers are mentally fit, they are more alert, focused, and capable of responding to incidents with clarity and composure.

Learning to recognize the trauma, find non-destructive coping mechanisms, and seek professional assistance is a unique journey for everyone. There's no one-size-fits-all approach. However, here are some practical strategies that can help:

- Acknowledge your experience.
    - Don't try to suppress or deny your feelings.

- Talk about it.
    - Share your experience with someone you trust.

- Seek professional help.
    - A therapist can provide you with tools and techniques for managing your trauma.

- Engage in self-care.
    - Make time for activities that bring you joy and relaxation.

- Practice mindfulness.
    - Mindfulness exercises can help you stay present in the moment and reduce stress.

The positive ripple effects of prioritizing mental health extend beyond individual officers. When law enforcement agencies implement comprehensive mental health programs, they set a precedent for other organizations and sectors to follow. This can contribute to a broader cultural shift that recognizes the importance of mental health in all professions, encouraging a more holistic approach to well-being in society as a whole.

When we give them the permission and encouragement to practice self-care and make their mental health a top priority, they not only enhance their own resilience and performance but also create a positive impact on their communities. Fostering a culture that values mental well-being, law enforcement agencies can ensure that their officers are equipped to serve effectively, ultimately leading to safer and healthier communities for everyone.

Breaking the Silence:
Building a Culture of Support

The concept of masculinity has long been intertwined with ideals of strength, stoicism, and self-reliance, particularly in fields such as law enforcement, where these traits are often glorified. However, it is essential to reexamine this traditional understanding of masculinity, especially in light of the unique challenges faced by law enforcement officers.

These ideals of masculinity are not confined to men alone; they extend across all genders within the profession.

Women in law enforcement, for instance, may find themselves navigating the same expectations of strength and emotional restraint, often having to prove their competence in a field that has historically been male-dominated. As a result, the celebration of these characteristics can create a paradox where individuals, regardless of gender, may feel compelled to conform to a narrow definition of what it means to be successful in their roles.

The pressures of the job, including exposure to trauma, high-stress situations, and the need to maintain authority, can create an environment where seeking help is perceived as a weakness.

Seeking help is often the stigma surrounding mental health. We are taught that showing weakness is a sign of being less of a person. However, it is important to challenge this societal norm and understand that seeking help is not a sign of weakness.

It takes great strength and courage to acknowledge that you need support and to reach out for it. By recognizing the importance of seeking assistance, we can redefine masculinity to include emotional intelligence, resilience, and the courage to be vulnerable. This shift not only benefits us, as individuals within law enforcement, but also enhances the overall effectiveness of the organization.

When officers feel empowered to seek help for mental health issues, stress management, or personal struggles, they are more likely to perform their duties effectively and maintain their well-being.

In reality, we know this is not an easy task. Taking the first step is very hard because we don't know who to trust and what will happen if we do reach out for help. Will it be the end of me as a person? What will people think of me? Will I lose my job, my family, my life as I know it?

When I talked about the final fall of my resiliency and my thoughts of ending the pain, when I was outside and walking in that circle, for what seemed to be an eternity, I was not thinking about how I could get better, they were about how my life would change from the perspective of others around me.

What was the next step, I did not know what to do or who to call. I felt like I was losing my mind. I could not focus on anything else, my palms were sweating, my heart was racing, and I felt like I was about to pass out. How do I make this stop? I just wanted that feeling to stop!

In speaking with a therapist after the fact, I found that at that moment, we often fail to recognize that our reluctance to seek assistance places us at risk of losing what we hold dear. Our attention is primarily directed towards how we want others to see us, rather than exploring avenues to end our suffering. I was at a crossroads and in ending that suffering I only saw two options, get help, or make it go away forever. Help is what I choose.

Reaching out for help is a sign of self-awareness and taking responsibility for your well-being. It shows that you are willing to put in the effort to improve your mental health and overall quality of life.

Seeking help is not a sign of failure, but rather a sign of resilience and determination to overcome any obstacles that may come your way. So, let go of the stigma and know that seeking help is a positive step towards a healthier and happier you.

Acknowledging the importance of your health and well-being is a crucial step in personal development. It involves understanding that you are the primary agent in your life, responsible for making choices that enhance your physical, emotional, and mental wellness.

> *"Treat yourself with the same kindness and respect you would treat someone who has been victimized. Give it back to yourself."* – Barbara Rubel

Taking charge of your health and welfare empowers you to take the necessary action to seek out the resources and support systems that can enhance your quality of life. You begin to see that all the questions and loyalties you thought would destroy you if you reached out for help, become the strength and stability in your life once again.

When you embrace this responsibility, you begin to lay the groundwork for a more fulfilling and balanced existence.

Here's what you can do to help break the silence:

- Talk openly about mental health.
    - Start by having conversations with your peers, your family, and your friends, having open and honest conversations with your peers, family, and friends, we can create a support system that helps us through difficult times.

- Be a supportive friend.
  - Being a supportive friend involves actively listening to our colleagues and encouraging them during challenging times. This will foster a sense of trust and camaraderie but also create an environment where individuals feel valued and understood.
  - When we are able to truly hear their concerns and validate their feelings, we contribute to their emotional well-being and help them navigate through difficulties more effectively.
- Seek out resources
  - We must also be willing to seek out resources for ourselves and others, whether it is through your department or outside organizations. There are numerous resources available to help us cope with the stress and trauma of our job.
  - Take advantage of these resources and not try to handle everything on your own. There are numerous resources available to law enforcement officers who are struggling with their mental health.

As law enforcement officers, we take an oath to serve and protect our communities. However, this commitment to duty often comes at the cost of our mental health. It is important to recognize that we are not alone in this struggle.

Organizational Support

Change cannot originate not only from the officers but also from the organization itself, which needs to foster an environment that emphasizes and encourages mental health support and overall wellness. Leadership must take an active role in creating a culture where mental health is prioritized and openly discussed.

To achieve this, organizations can implement comprehensive training programs for all employees, including management, to raise awareness about mental health issues and reduce stigma. These programs should focus on recognizing signs of mental distress, understanding the importance of mental well-being, and learning how to provide support to colleagues in need.

Establish clear policies that promote work-life balance, such as flexible working hours, remote work options, and adequate time off for mental health days. By normalizing the conversation around mental health and allowing employees to take the necessary time to recharge, organizations can create a more supportive atmosphere.

Remember, we are all in this together. The thin blue line is a reminder of our shared commitment to protect and serve, but it also serves as a reminder to take care of ourselves and each other.

Mental health is just as important as physical health, and it's up to us to create a culture where seeking help is encouraged and supported. Let's break the stigma surrounding mental health in law enforcement and support each other in our journey towards overall well-being.

No matter what has occurred in your life up to this point, it should have no bearing at all on how you live from now on.' That you, living in the here and now, are the one who determines your own life."

— *Ichiro Kishimi, The Courage to Be Disliked: How to Free Yourself, Change Your Life and Achieve Real Happiness*

The Constant Battle Within

The air hung heavy with the smell of stale coffee and burnt toast as I stared out the window, my reflection a blurry, haggard version of the man I used to be. The years that I have spent as a career first responder had brought unexpected challenges, the quiet solitude a stark contrast to the frenetic pace of my life on the force.

"You're letting the memories get to you again, aren't you?" my wife's voice, cutting through the haze, her gentle touch on my shoulder snapping me back to reality.

I let out a weary sigh, turning to meet her worried gaze. She is my partner in life, my confidante, and now, my unwavering pillar of support as I navigate this new phase.

"Just… thinking," I muttered, feeling a familiar knot of anxiety constricting my chest.

"About the case?" she asked, in her voice soft.

I nodded, the details of that night replaying in my mind like a cruel, recurring nightmare. The young woman, her face pale and lifeless, the fear etched onto the faces of her loved ones. It was a case that had haunted me, a dark stain on the fabric of my memory.

"I'm trying to move on," I said, my voice cracking slightly. "But it's hard."

She squeezed my hand, her eyes full of understanding. "I know," she said. "And that's why it's so important to take care of yourself."

It was a reminder I needed to hear, a reminder I knew all too well. During my years in police work, self-care was a luxury I could rarely afford. The adrenaline, the constant pressure, the fear – they all fueled me, a dangerous cocktail that fueled my drive and, ultimately, my internal destruction.

"You know," she continued, "it's like you said back then – we're all wearing the same blue line, but we're not all equipped to handle the weight of it."

Her words echoed in my mind, bringing back a memory of a conversation we'd had years ago. Back then, I'd dismissed the idea of self-care as frivolous, a luxury for those who weren't hardened by the reality of the streets.

"But it's not about being weak," she said, her voice filled with warmth. "It's about being strong enough to know when you need help, to prioritize your well-being."

I'd always believed that self-care was for the weak, a luxury I couldn't afford while working the streets. But as I sat there, surrounded by memories of my past, I realized that prioritizing my well-being wasn't a sign of weakness. It took strength to admit when I needed help and to take care of myself.

As the years of my career grew longer it had been a hard lesson, one that taught me the importance of self-care. I knew I couldn't continue to ignore my own needs and pretend that the emotional toll of the job didn't affect me. It was time for me to find new tools and strategies to manage the weight of my past and the trauma it had left behind. I needed to learn how to put my well-being first, without feeling guilty or weak.

Sitting there in that moment, I realized that self-care is necessary part of being a strong and resilient person. It was about recognizing when I needed help and prioritizing my own mental and emotional health. And as I looked towards the future, I knew that taking care of myself would not only benefit me but also those around me.

Coming to terms with this difficult lesson was a significant turning point for me, one that I had resisted for far too long while trying to bury the trauma and stress that had haunted me throughout my life. For years, I had convinced myself that I could simply push through the pain, ignoring the emotional weight that clung to me like a shadow. I thought that by burying my feelings deep within, I could avoid confronting the uncomfortable truths that lay beneath the surface. However, this approach only led to a cycle of avoidance and denial, leaving me feeling increasingly overwhelmed and disconnected from my own emotions.

Now, as I confronted the shadows of my past, it became clear that I needed to equip myself with fresh tools and strategies to navigate the emotional challenges that my work demanded. I realized that the old ways of coping—whether it was through distraction, denial, or unhealthy habits—were no longer serving me. Instead, I needed to embrace a new mindset, one that acknowledged my pain and allowed me to process it in a healthy way.

In recognizing the importance of developing healthier coping mechanisms. I began to explore mindfulness practices, such as meditation and journaling, which provided me with a safe space to reflect on my feelings and experiences. This not only helped me to ground myself in the present moment but also allowed me to gain clarity on the patterns and triggers that had previously controlled my reactions. I learned to approach my emotions with curiosity rather than judgment, fostering a sense of compassion for myself that had long been absent.

Mindfulness and Meditation

"Mindfulness?" My colleague, Matt, had scoffed when I'd first mentioned the idea. "Isn't that some hippie mumbo jumbo?" (you mention Matt many times so I would share a bit more about him "best friend, confidant, etc.)

"Not exactly," I'd countered, my voice laced with a newfound conviction. "It's about being present, being aware of your thoughts and feelings without judgment."

Mindfulness and meditation were the new tools I needed to effectively manage the emotional toll of my job and my past experiences. They allowed me to step back from the chaos and observe my thoughts and feelings without being consumed by them.

With mindfulness, I learned to be present in the moment, to focus on my breath, and release any negative thoughts or emotions that arose. It was not an easy practice, but gradually I was able to let go of the weight I had been carrying for so long. Meditation, on the other hand, gave me the space and clarity to reflect on my experiences and find peace within myself.

It was a process of self-discovery and self-compassion, as I learned to be kind to myself and let go of any guilt or shame. These new strategies not only helped me manage the emotional toll of my job but also allowed me to better understand and cope with my past traumas. I no longer felt overwhelmed or helpless in the face of difficult emotions. Instead, I had the tools to face them head-on and find peace within myself.

Mindfulness and meditation had become an integral part of my healing journey, and I was grateful for the new perspective and strength they had given me. Mindfulness, I had learned, was a powerful tool for managing stress. It allowed you to take a step back from the chaos, to observe your thoughts and feelings without getting swept away by them.

"Imagine you're holding a cup of hot coffee," I explained to Matt, as I demonstrated a simple mindfulness exercise. "Focus on the sensation of the warmth in your hand, the aroma of the coffee, the taste on your tongue."

Matt, initially skeptical, had cautiously joined in, his eyes narrowing in concentration.

"It's... kind of weird," he admitted after a few minutes, his face contorted with a strange mix of discomfort and intrigue.

"That's because it's different," I chuckled. "It's about shifting your focus from the outside world to the inside."

Matt had continued to practice mindfulness with me, and I could see a gradual shift in his demeanor. The tension in his shoulders seemed to ease, his quick temper less volatile.

Meditation, I explained, was another way to cultivate a sense of inner peace. It was a practice of focusing your attention on a single point, be it your breath, a mantra, or a visual image.

"It sounds like a lot of work," Matt had grumbled, his natural aversion to anything that seemed passive challenging his growing interest.

"It takes practice, Matt," I had acknowledged. "But even a few minutes of focused meditation each day can make a difference."

Meditation had been a lifesaver for me, allowing me to ground myself in the present moment, to quiet the cacophony of thoughts that often plagued my mind.

"You know," Matt said one afternoon, his voice a touch softer than usual, "I've been trying this mindfulness thing. It's not bad."

It was a small victory, a sign that even the most resistant among us could be swayed by the power of self-care.

Journaling and Reflection

Matt's revelation about mindfulness sparked my interest. I, too, have been struggling with negative thoughts and emotions that often plague my mind. His small victory gave me hope that maybe I could also find some peace through self-care. I decided to give it a try, starting with journaling and reflection.

Writing down my thoughts and feelings allowed me to acknowledge them and understand them better. I was able to identify patterns and triggers, which helped me find ways to cope and manage them. Through journaling, I also learned the importance of self-reflection. It allowed me to pause and look within myself, rather than constantly looking outside for validation and answers. I discovered things about myself that I never knew before, and it helped me grow and become more self-aware.

"So, you're telling me I should write down my feelings?" My friend, Steve, had laughed when I'd first mentioned journaling. "Isn't that a little… girly?"

Steve, a seasoned detective himself, had always been more of a "bottle it up" kind of guy. Sharing his emotions was seen as a weakness, a sign that he wasn't cut out for the job.

"It's not about being girly, Steve," I countered, my voice firm. "It's about processing, about getting the thoughts and feelings out of your head and onto paper."

Journaling was a powerful tool for self-reflection, a way to confront your emotions and understand the patterns of your thoughts.

"Think of it like a private conversation with yourself," I explained, pulling out my trusty leather-bound journal. "A place where you can be honest, where you can let everything out without judgment."

Steve, despite his initial skepticism, had agreed to try it. He'd been hesitant at first, his words stilted and guarded. But as he continued to write, a transformation began to take hold.

"You know," he admitted one evening, his voice subdued, "It feels kind of good to get all of this out."

Journaling had allowed Steve to process the traumatic events he'd witnessed on the job, to confront the fear and anger that had festered beneath the surface. He'd started to see the benefits of expressing his emotions, of acknowledging the impact of his experiences.

"It's like a weight lifted off my shoulders," he confessed, his eyes revealing a newfound sense of peace.

"And that's what self-care is all about, Steve," I said, feeling a surge of pride. "It's about taking care of your mental and emotional well-being, so you can be the best version of yourself."

Exercise and Physical Activity

"Who has time for the gym?" My old friend, Al, had snorted when I suggested exercise as a way to manage stress. "We're all too busy running around chasing criminals."

Al, a man who lived and breathed law enforcement, had always been skeptical of anything that didn't involve a badge and a gun. He'd seen firsthand the physical toll the job took on his colleagues, the injuries, the fatigue, the burnout.

"It's not about becoming a fitness guru, Al" I countered, my voice calm. "It's about finding an activity you enjoy, something that allows you to move your body and release endorphins."

Al's skepticism was a common sentiment among those in our line of work. Long hours, unpredictable schedules, and the constant pressure we faced left little room for self-care. Yet, I knew that neglecting our physical health only added to the strain, often exacerbating the very stress we sought to escape.

"It's about finding an outlet, Al," I continued, my voice steady. "Something to help you blow off steam and clear your head. It could be a run, a game of basketball, or even a walk. You know, fresh air and some sunlight can do wonders for a person."

The memory of a colleague, his once-robust frame now frail and weakened by illness, flashed before me. It was a stark reminder of the consequences of neglecting our health.

"You have to take care of yourself, my friend," I urged. "Your body and mind are your most important tools in this job." Al's resistance began to waver, his curiosity piqued. "Alright, I'll give it a shot," he conceded. "Maybe a jog in the mornings before shift. Can't hurt to try, right?"

A smile spread across my face, knowing that Al had taken the first step towards a healthier, more balanced life. It was a step that many in our profession struggled to take, often to their detriment. Yet, with each small victory, we chipped away at the stigma surrounding self-care, fostering a culture that valued resilience and well-being. Exercise, I knew from personal experience, could be a powerful antidote to stress. It helped to release endorphins, which had mood-boosting effects, and it could reduce tension in the muscles, helping to relieve physical and emotional stress.

"I used to jog every morning before work," I shared with Joel, my voice a touch nostalgic. "It was my way of starting the day with a clear head."

Joel, a man who prided himself on his physical prowess, had begrudgingly agreed to give it a try. He'd started with short walks around the neighborhood, gradually increasing the distance and intensity as he felt his body and mind responding to the change.

"You know," he admitted one morning, his face flushed from a run, "It's not bad. I feel better."

Joel had started to see the benefits of exercise, not just for his physical health, but for his mental well-being too. He'd discovered a new outlet for his energy, a way to release the pent-up tension that came with his job.

"It's not about being perfect, Joel," I said, my voice filled with understanding. "It's about finding a way to move your body that works for you." No matter what you choose to do at least you're doing something to occupy your mind and make you feel much better about yourself".

Exercise, I knew, was a crucial part of any self-care routine. It wasn't just about physical fitness; it was about mental and emotional well-being.

"So," I said, my voice turning serious, "what are you going to do to take care of yourself today?"

Matt, Steve, and Al exchanged glances, their expressions a mixture of contemplation and determination.

"I'm going to go for a run," Al declared, his voice laced with newfound confidence.

"I'm going to write in my journal," Steve announced, his eyes gleaming with a hint of excitement.

"I'm going to try that mindfulness thing again," Matt admitted, a reluctant smile playing on his lips.

As they headed off, I couldn't help but smile. Gone were the days of neglecting themselves, and ignoring the toll that their jobs had taken on them. I could see it in their eyes, the newfound determination to take care of their physical and mental well-being. It was a ray of hope in a world that often seemed bleak and unforgiving. Al's declaration to go for a run showed his newfound confidence, a sign that he was finally taking control of his life.

Steve's excitement to write in his journal was a reminder that self-reflection was just as important as the work they did. Matt's admission to trying mindfulness again, despite his initial reluctance, showed that he was willing to put in the effort to find inner peace. As I watched them leave, I couldn't help but think that perhaps these small steps towards self-care would lead to bigger changes in their lives. Maybe they would finally find the balance between their duty and their own needs. And as a brother officer, I couldn't be prouder to see my comrades prioritize their well-being. It gave me hope that we could all heal from the traumas we had endured and come out stronger on the other side.

These men, the men I'd served alongside, the men who had witnessed the darkest corners of humanity, were finally starting to prioritize their well-being.

The Journey of Self-Care

As I watched my colleagues focus on their well-being, I couldn't help but feel a sense of pride and relief. For so long, self-care was not even a thought in the minds of police officers and first responders.

The mission and the well-being of others always came first. But now, seeing them take the time to heal and prioritize themselves, I knew that our time together had not been in vain. The journey of self-care was a difficult one, but it was worth it.

The trauma we had endured during our time in service was not something that could be easily brushed off. It left deep scars that needed time and effort to heal. But the fact that we were now on this journey together, supporting and encouraging each other, made all the difference. We were no longer just officers, but a band of brothers and sisters who had gone through the worst together and were now emerging even stronger.

It was a reminder that self-care was not a sign of weakness, but an act of strength and resilience. As we continued on this journey, I had hope that we would all come out on the other side, not just as survivors, but as individuals who had grown and evolved through our experiences.

The road to self-care may have been a difficult one, but it was one that we were now navigating together, and that makes all the difference. The road to self-care is not easy, I know that. It will be a constant battle, a daily struggle to prioritize your own needs in a world that often demands so much. "But it's worth it," I thought to myself, the weight of my past experiences heavy on my heart. "Every step, every small act of self-care, brings you closer to a place of peace, a place of resilience."

And as I sat there, watching the sun sink below the horizon, casting long shadows across the town, I felt a flicker of hope. Perhaps, just perhaps, this was the beginning of a new chapter, a chapter filled with self-discovery, self-acceptance, and the promise of a brighter future.

I stood up, my resolve solidifying with every breath I took. I had come too far, learned too much, to let the darkness consume me. It was time to step into the light, embrace the journey of self-care, and find my path to resilience.

As I walked towards the door, my phone buzzed in my pocket. The name on the screen sent a jolt of fear through my body. It was Detective James, the lead investigator on the case that had haunted me for years.

"Chris," James's voice crackled through the phone, "We've got a lead. You need to come down to the station. It's important."

A wave of dread washed over me, my heart pounding in my chest. This was it, the moment of truth. But as I glanced at my wife, her hand gently squeezing mine, I knew I wouldn't face it alone. I had the tools, the strategies, and the support system I needed to navigate the darkness, to find the strength to move forward.

I took a deep breath, the scent of coffee and burnt toast suddenly fading into the background as the weight of the moment settled upon me.

"I'm coming," I said, my voice steady despite the tremor in my hand.

This was the moment I had been preparing for, the moment I had been dreading. But I was ready. I was ready to face the ghosts of my past, to confront the demons that had haunted me for so long.

I was ready to fight for my peace, for my resilience, for my future.

The future.

And as I stepped out into the night, the city lights blurring into a dazzling kaleidoscope of colors, I wondered what lay ahead. Would I find justice for the victims? Would I finally be able to lay the ghosts of my past to rest?

Only time will tell.

Building A Support System

As a member of the law enforcement community, it can be easy to feel isolated and alone in dealing with the emotional toll of the job. The weight of the badge can be heavy, both physically and mentally, as it represents the sacrifices and responsibilities that come with serving and protecting the public. However, it is important to remember that you are not alone in this struggle.

It is common for those in law enforcement to experience invisible wounds, such as post-traumatic stress disorder (PTSD) and depression, as a result of constant exposure to traumatic events and high levels of stress. These silent battles can often go unnoticed and unaddressed, leading to a downward spiral of mental health issues. That is why it is crucial to recognize the warning signs and have the necessary tools to manage the storm that comes with the job.

But even with these tools, it is still a daunting task to face these challenges alone. That is why it is important to reach out to others for support and to remind yourself that you don't have to fight this alone. Whether it's seeking help from a therapist or talking to a trusted colleague, having a support system can make all the difference in managing the invisible wounds of the job. Remember, it takes strength and courage to ask for help, and it is a sign of resilience, not weakness. You are not alone, and together, we can face these challenges head-on.

Imagine this: You're on a late-night shift, a tense domestic dispute escalates, and you find yourself caught in the crossfire of emotions. You de-escalate the situation, but the adrenaline lingers, the fear, the frustration. The next day, at the station, the silence of the breakroom echoes your internal turmoil. You might not want to burden your colleagues, but those unspoken struggles can feel isolating.

This is where the power of connection comes in. It's not just about having people around; it's about having those who understand the unique pressures of the job. Those who have seen the darkness felt the burden and emerged with strength. These are the individuals who can truly empathize with your experiences and offer support and guidance. They know the weight that comes with the job and can provide a sense of camaraderie and understanding that is crucial for mental health and wellness. In the often high-stress environment of emergency response work, it's essential to have a support system, both on and off the job.

These connections can help you process and cope with the difficult emotions that can come with the territory. And while it may be challenging to open up and share your struggles, the power of connection lies in the fact that you are not alone. Together, you and your colleagues can navigate the ups and downs of the job and emerge stronger and more resilient.

Think of your support system as a lifeline. A network of individuals who stand by you, who listen without judgment, and who offer a shoulder to lean on.

Building Meaningful Relationships

The first step in building a strong support system is recognizing the importance of relationships. You can't be an island.

An essential first step in creating a strong support network is recognizing the importance of relationships. This acknowledgment goes beyond surface-level awareness; it entails a profound understanding of the diverse roles that relationships play in our lives.

Relationships are not merely social constructs; they are fundamental to our emotional health and personal growth. By appreciating the value of these connections, we establish a solid groundwork for developing a network that can offer emotional, social, and practical support when necessary.

When we prioritize the relationships we build with others, we foster an environment where mutual support can thrive. This environment is marked by open communication, trust, and a willingness to be vulnerable. It enables us to share our challenges and successes, secure in the knowledge that we have people who genuinely care about our well-being.

The advantages of such connections are numerous; they provide emotional support during tough times, motivation to pursue our aspirations, and shared experiences that enrich our lives. Some of those that we develop these relationships include those we interact with each and every day.

- Friends and Family:
    - Reach out to those who genuinely care about you. Open communication is crucial. They might not understand the specifics of your job, but they can offer emotional support, a listening ear, and a distraction from the pressures you face.

- Colleagues:
    - Your fellow officers are your brothers and sisters in arms. They've walked a similar path, facing similar challenges. Create a culture of open dialogue and mutual support within your department. Share your experiences, listen to theirs, and don't be afraid to ask for help when you need it.

- Mentors:
    - Having a senior officer, you respect and trust can be invaluable. They can provide

guidance, offer a different perspective, and help you navigate difficult situations.

- Peer Support Groups:
    - These groups are specifically designed for law enforcement officers to connect and share their experiences. They offer a safe space for emotional support, validation, and a sense of community.

Seeking Professional Help: Breaking the Stigma:

We need to confront the reality: there is a considerable stigma surrounding mental health in law enforcement that poses a major obstacle to the well-being of officers and the effectiveness of the entire department. This stigma often stems from a culture that values toughness, resilience, and self-sufficiency above all else. Officers are conditioned to believe that they must be able to handle their issues on their own, to push through pain and adversity without showing vulnerability. This mindset can create an environment where individuals feel isolated and reluctant to seek help, fearing judgment from their peers or concerns about their professional reputation.

Its time, time to change the culture of how we look at mental health in this profession. Transforming the perception of mental health among law enforcement officers and first responders is not just important; it is essential for the well-being of these individuals and the communities they serve.

The perception of mental health in law enforcement and first response is about more than just addressing individual needs; it is about creating a resilient workforce that can effectively serve and protect our communities. By prioritizing mental health, we not only support the well-being of these brave individuals but also enhance the overall safety and health of society as a whole. It takes immense bravery to confront one's struggles and to reach out for support, especially in a field where the expectation is often to remain stoic and unyielding.

There is value in creating a culture that prioritizes mental health within these organizations. Leadership must actively promote open discussions about mental health, encouraging officers to share their experiences without fear of judgment or repercussions. By fostering an environment of trust and understanding, we can help individuals feel safe in seeking help and support through therapy and counseling.

- Therapy and Counseling:
    - A therapist can provide a structured and confidential space to explore your thoughts, emotions, and experiences. They can offer tools and strategies for coping with stress, trauma, and anxiety. They can

also help you develop healthy coping mechanisms and build resilience.

- Finding a therapist:
    - If you're considering therapy, it's essential to find a therapist who specializes in working with first responders. They understand the specific challenges you face and can provide tailored support. Your department's Employee Assistance Program (EAP) can be a great resource for finding a qualified therapist.

Acknowledging that you genuinely deserve support when necessary is a vital aspect of self-care. Mental health is just as important as physical health, and neglecting it can lead to serious consequences, both personally and professionally. By breaking down the barriers of stigma and encouraging open conversations about mental health, we can create an environment where officers feel safe to express their struggles and seek the help they need.

Finding Your Tribe: Building a Network of Support:

Finding your tribe is a crucial part of building a network of support. While your family, colleagues, and therapist can provide valuable assistance, there is something unique about finding a community that truly understands your experiences.

This community, or "tribe", is a collective of individuals who share common experiences, challenges, or interests, fostering a unique bond among its members. These individuals often find themselves navigating similar life circumstances, whether they are related to personal struggles, professional hurdles, or shared passions. Within this tribe, members can offer each other empathy, guidance, and support, creating a nurturing environment where everyone feels valued and understood.

Belonging to such a tribe is particularly significant for those who may feel isolated or misunderstood in their experiences. In a world that can often feel disconnected and overwhelming, having a group of like-minded individuals can provide a crucial sense of acceptance and belonging. This feeling of being part of something larger than oneself can be incredibly empowering, as it reassures individuals that they are not alone in their struggles. The shared experiences within the tribe foster a deep sense of camaraderie, allowing members to relate to one another on a profound level.

The supportive network that constitutes a tribe can take many forms. It may include friends who have stood by each other through thick and thin, colleagues who understand the pressures of a demanding work environment, or even participants in online support groups that transcend geographical boundaries. Regardless of the specific makeup of the tribe, the common thread is the creation of a safe space where individuals can express their thoughts and feelings without fear of judgment. Things such as support groups and online communities can help to facilitate this "tribal" network.

- Support Groups:
    o There are numerous support groups for law enforcement officers nationwide. These groups offer a space for shared experiences, mutual support, and a sense of belonging.

- Online Communities:
    o There are also online communities where officers can connect with others who understand the challenges of the job. These virtual spaces can provide a sense of community and support, even when you're feeling isolated.

This shared understanding and connection can be profoundly reassuring. Members of the tribe often find solace in knowing that others have faced similar challenges and have emerged stronger on the other side. They can share coping strategies, offer advice, and provide emotional support during difficult times.

This exchange of experiences not only helps individuals navigate their own journeys but also strengthens the bonds within the tribe, creating a resilient community that thrives on mutual support.

Fostering a Culture of Support and Acceptance

Building a strong support system is not a one-time event; it's an ongoing process. We all have a responsibility to create a culture of support and acceptance within our law enforcement community which involves creating a comprehensive system that includes access to mental health professionals, peer support programs, and wellness resources.

This network should be designed to provide officers with the tools they need to cope with the unique stresses of their job, as well as to promote overall well-being. It is essential for law enforcement agencies to prioritize mental health as a core component of their operational framework, integrating it into training, policies, and daily practices.

This endeavor involves several key components that, when woven together, create a rich tapestry of encouragement and inclusivity.

Open Communication

Open lines of communication are essential for building trust and understanding among team members.

Encouraging officers to share their thoughts, concerns, and experiences without fear of judgment or reprisal is crucial. Regular meetings, feedback sessions, and anonymous surveys can provide platforms for dialogue, allowing individuals to voice their opinions and contribute to the collective well-being of the department. By actively listening to one another, we can identify areas for improvement and celebrate successes, reinforcing a sense of belonging.

> Active Listening:
> When a colleague opens up about their struggles, listen without judgment. Offer support and understanding.
>
> Positive Reinforcement:
> Recognize and appreciate officers who reach out for help. Acknowledge their courage and resilience.

Creating Support Systems

Establishing formal and informal support systems is vital for fostering a culture of encouragement. Peer support programs, counseling services, and wellness initiatives can provide officers with the resources they need to navigate the challenges of their roles. Encouraging camaraderie through team-building activities and social events can also strengthen relationships among officers, creating a sense of unity and shared purpose. When individuals know they have a support network to rely on, they are more likely to thrive both personally and professionally.

Building a strong support system not only benefits the individual officers but also contributes to the overall well-being of the entire law enforcement community. It is important to recognize the importance of support and acceptance and actively work towards creating a culture that prioritizes the mental health of our officers.

Encouraging Professional Development

Investing in the professional growth of officers is a powerful way to demonstrate support and commitment to their success. Providing access to training, mentorship programs, and career advancement opportunities empowers individuals to reach their full potential. By recognizing and celebrating achievements, whether big or small, we create an environment where officers feel valued and motivated to excel. This commitment to development not only enhances individual performance but also strengthens the overall effectiveness of the department.

Promoting Diversity and Representation

A truly inclusive environment recognizes and values the diverse backgrounds, perspectives, and experiences of its members. Law enforcement agencies should strive to recruit individuals from various demographics, ensuring that the workforce reflects the community it serves. This diversity not only enhances problem-solving and decision-making but also fosters empathy and understanding among officers. Training programs that emphasize cultural competency and bias awareness can further support this initiative, equipping officers with the tools to engage effectively with all community members.

Remember, you don't have to carry the weight of the world alone. Building a strong support system is crucial for the well-being of police officers.

In addition to the physical and mental demands of the job, officers also have to deal with the emotional toll that comes with protecting and serving their communities. This is where the importance of support and a sense of belonging comes into play.

For meaningful change to occur, it is crucial that the organization as a whole embraces the importance of mental health and wellness. This requires a commitment from all levels of the organization, from top leadership to individual employees, to work collaboratively towards creating a healthier, more supportive workplace. By doing so, organizations not only enhance the well-being of their employees but also improve overall productivity, morale, and job satisfaction.

A Roadmap to Resilience
Creating a Wellness Routine

Building a consistent wellness routine is essential for developing lasting resilience. It's not about being perfect, but rather finding what works best for you.

This journey is unique to each individual, and there is no one-size-fits-all formula. Think of this chapter as a guidebook for navigating the mental health journey, providing you with a personalized roadmap for resilience. Incorporating practices that nourish your mind, body, and spirit is crucial for maintaining a healthy and resilient lifestyle. This routine doesn't have to be overwhelming; it can start with small, manageable steps.

> *"Resilience isn't a single skill. It's a variety of skills and coping mechanisms. To bounce back from bumps in the road as well as failures, you should focus on emphasizing the positive." —Jean Chatzky*

Maybe it's taking a few minutes each morning to meditate or going for a walk in nature. Whatever it may be, finding what works for you is key. Remember, this journey is not about reaching a destination; it's about creating a sustainable and fulfilling lifestyle. As you continue on this journey, be patient with yourself, and don't be afraid to adjust your routine as needed. Your wellness routine is a tool for building resilience, and it will evolve and change as you do. Embrace the process and trust that you are on the right path towards a healthier and happier self.

This routine isn't about becoming a health guru overnight; it's about incorporating practices that nourish your mind, body, and spirit. Here's a framework to get you started:

- Mindfulness:
  We've explored the power of mindfulness throughout this book. Take a moment each day, perhaps during a commute or before bed, to simply observe your breath. Feel the rise and fall of your chest, the air moving in and out of your nostrils. Let go of any thoughts that distract you, gently bringing your attention back to your breath.

- Journaling:
  Journaling is a powerful tool for processing emotions and gaining self-awareness. Set aside time, even just 15 minutes, to write down your thoughts and feelings. Don't censor yourself. Let the words flow freely, whether it's about a stressful encounter, a moment of gratitude, or simply what you had for breakfast.

- Exercise:
  Physical activity is a proven stress reliever and mood booster. Aim for at least 30 minutes of

moderate-intensity exercise most days of the week. It could be a brisk walk, a run, a yoga session, or anything that gets your heart rate up and makes you feel good.

- Healthy Relationships:
  Don't underestimate the power of connection. Spend quality time with loved ones, nurture friendships, and join groups or activities that bring you joy. Social interaction is essential for our mental well-being.

- Seeking Help:
  Remember, there's no shame in seeking professional help when you need it. A therapist or counselor can provide a safe and supportive space to work through challenges and develop coping skills.

Embracing the Journey

Resilience is not a destination; it's a journey. It's important to remember that the journey towards resilience isn't always easy. There will be bumps along the way, but you should never give up. The challenges you face will only make you stronger and more resilient in the end. This journey is about growth, learning, and becoming the best version of yourself.

To successfully embrace this journey, it's important to engage in activities that bring you joy. This can be anything from spending time with loved ones, pursuing a hobby, or simply taking a walk in nature. These activities will help you build your resilience and give you the strength to overcome any obstacles that come your way.

Additionally, social interaction is essential for our mental well-being. Surrounding yourself with supportive and positive people can make a world of difference in your journey towards resilience.

Remember, there's no shame in seeking professional help when you need it. A therapist or counselor can provide a safe and supportive space to work through challenges and develop coping skills. This journey is not meant to be taken alone, and seeking help is a sign of strength, not weakness. Embrace this journey towards resilience, and know that with each step you take, you are growing and becoming stronger.

Self-Compassion:
> Treat yourself with the same kindness and understanding you would offer a friend. Be patient with yourself, acknowledge your efforts, and celebrate even the smallest victories.

Continuous Self-Improvement:
> Resilience is an ongoing process. It requires constant attention and effort. Be willing to experiment with new practices, seek feedback, and adjust your approach as needed.

Continuing the Conversation

The most important aspect of building resilience by creating a culture of open dialogue and support within the law enforcement community. Encouraging officers to openly discuss their experiences and seek support from their colleagues, creates a sense of camaraderie and strengthens the overall resilience of the team. This also allows for continuous learning and growth, as officers can share their best practices and learn from one another's experiences.

Start the Conversation:
    Share your experiences with colleagues and friends. Let them know it's okay to struggle, to ask for help, and to prioritize their mental well-being.

Be a Supportive Listener:
    Listen attentively when your colleagues open up. Offer a kind word, a listening ear, or resources that can help.

Create a Culture of Support:
    Work together to break down the stigma surrounding mental health. Encourage your department or agency to offer resources and training on mental wellness.

While it may seem daunting to constantly work on building resilience, it is important to celebrate even the smallest victories along the way. Acknowledging one's efforts and recognizing the progress made can provide motivation and encouragement to continue on the path of self-improvement.

By making resilience an ongoing conversation and prioritizing it within the law enforcement community, officers can better equip themselves to handle any challenges that may arise.

By prioritizing discussions around resilience, law enforcement agencies can create an environment where officers feel supported and empowered to address the psychological and emotional demands of their work.

This ongoing conversation can take many forms, including workshops, training sessions, and peer support groups, all aimed at equipping officers with the tools and strategies necessary to build their resilience. Such initiatives can help officers develop coping mechanisms for stress, trauma, and the high-pressure situations they often encounter.

If we strive to normalizing discussions about mental health and resilience, agencies can reduce the stigma associated with seeking help, encouraging officers to reach out when they need support.

Looking Ahead

We all face challenges and hardships in our daily lives, and sometimes, it can feel overwhelming. In a fast-paced work environment, it's important to remember to take care of our mental health.

This book serves as a starting point to help build resilience and navigate through these challenges. It provides a solid foundation for individuals to embark on their journey towards mental wellness. Embracing the challenges and celebrating the victories along the way is crucial.

It's important to never stop learning and to continuously seek out resources and support. This can help create a culture of support within the workplace, breaking down the stigma surrounding mental health. By encouraging our departments or agencies to offer resources and training on mental wellness, we can all work together toward a brighter future.

Remember, you are not alone on this journey. The book offers guidance and support, and there are also people around you who are willing to listen and help.

With the right tools and a positive mindset, we can all take steps towards a healthier and happier life. The journey may not always be easy, but it is worth taking.

Let this book be your guide and know that a brighter future awaits. Embrace the challenges, celebrate the victories, and never stop learning.

Many officers fear the stigma and consequences that may come with seeking help for their mental health. This fear is often amplified by the "tough" and "macho" culture prevalent in law enforcement. Therefore, we must create a supportive and understanding environment where seeking help is not seen as a weakness, but rather a strength.

This can be achieved by implementing mental health support programs within police departments and providing confidential resources for officers to seek help.

It is also important for law enforcement leaders to openly discuss and address mental health issues, breaking the silence and encouraging others to do the same. By doing so, we can create a culture where officers feel safe and supported in seeking the help they need. It is our responsibility to ensure that our law enforcement officers receive the care and understanding they deserve.

Ongoing training and education about mental health can empower officers to recognize the signs of distress in themselves and their colleagues. This proactive approach can lead to early intervention, which is often key to preventing more severe mental health crises.

Encouraging open dialogue and providing resources for self-care can further enhance the resilience of officers, enabling them to perform their duties effectively while maintaining their mental health. Ultimately, ensuring that police officers feel valued and supported in their mental health journeys is a collective responsibility. It requires collaboration among law enforcement agencies, mental health professionals, and the community at large.

By working together to create a supportive environment, we can help officers navigate the challenges they face, leading to healthier individuals and, consequently, a more effective and compassionate law enforcement system.

Let us strive towards creating a culture where seeking help is encouraged and where our law enforcement officers know they are not alone in their struggles.

Remember, you are not alone. There are resources and support available, you must choose to take that first step and with that step, a brighter future awaits.

YOU ARE NOT ALONE!

If you need help, if you are struggling, if you have thought or are thinking about suicide.

If you feel you're at immediate risk, reach out to a trusted friend, family member, or healthcare professional.

HELP IS AVAILABLE!

Please call a crisis hotline, such as the National Suicide Prevention Lifeline at 800-273-8255.
Text HOME to the Crisis Textline at 741741.

Call – 988 or Chat – 988lifeline.org

COPLINE – 1-800- 267-5463

If you are having a medical emergency or there is immediate danger of harm, call 911 and explain that you need support for a mental health crisis.

Acknowledgments

First and foremost, I want to express my love, respect, and gratitude to my wife Renee, and my son, Zach, for their patience and understanding. Your presence in my life has been a constant source of strength and inspiration, I Love you both, very much.

I extend my heartfelt love and gratitude to my second family, the Town of Cheswold Police Department and to my fellow officers, past and present, for their unwavering dedication and courage in the face of adversity. Your experiences have shaped this book and inspired me to speak out about the importance of mental well-being within the law enforcement community.

Thank you to the Town of Cheswold, particularly Sam and Shadina, for reaching out and appointing me as Chief of Police in 2013, and to everyone who has served as the Mayor and Council of this amazing town for their steadfast support of me and this police department over the years. It has been a wild ride.

A special thanks to my friend, Matthew Davis for his unwavering and continued support and encouragement throughout this journey. Your friendship, advice, and belief in my vision have been a constant source of motivation.

I am deeply humbled and grateful to the many individuals who have contributed to this book, my journey as a law enforcement officer, and have encouraged me to be a voice for those who are struggling and a mental health advocate for our first responder community and the law enforcement officers who put on that tin on every single day.

My appreciation to the mental health professionals who have guided me on my path to healing and resilience can never be over exaggerated or understated, you saved my life.

And last, but certainly not least - Thank you, Ernie and Barbara for your friendship and assistance in making this book a reality. Your expertise and compassion for all of us who struggle with our own personal mental health has been invaluable in helping me understand the unique challenges we all face and having the courage to find our way through the silence behind the blue wall.

Bibliography

Carroll, L. (1993). *Alice's Adventures in Wonderland.* Dover Publications.

Kishimi, I., & Koga, F. (2013). The courage to be disliked: the Japanese phenomenon that shows you how to change your life and achieve real happiness. Atria Books.

Rubel, B. & Palamara, J. (2023). Living Blue: Helping Law Enforcement Officers and Their Families Survive and Thrive from Recruitment to Retirement. Griefwork Center, Inc.

Suggested Resources

I have no financial relationship with any persons or websites listed here. They are just books and links to/from individuals I have found helpful in my journey to self-awareness and personal mental health and wellness.

Books

Greatness Beyond the Badge: The Three Key Principles for Self-Awareness – Michael Laidler

Emotional Survival for Law Enforcement: A Guide for Officers and Their Families Revised Edition 2021 – Dr. Kevin M. Gilmartin

Emotional Intelligence 2.0 – Travis Bradberry & Jean Graves

Mental Health & De-Escalation: A Guide for Law Enforcement Professionals (Real Cops Training, Book 1) – Ernest Stevens & Nicholas Ruggiero

The Courage to be Disliked: The Japanese Phenomenon That Shows You How to Change Your Life and Achieve Real Happiness - Ichiro Kishimi & Fumitake Koga

The Courage to Be Happy: Discover the Power of Positive Psychology and Choose Happiness Every Day - Ichiro Kishimi & Fumitake Koga

Websites & Hotlines

Survive First - https://survivefirst.us/

Lighthouse Health & Wellness - https://www.lighthousehw.org/

Trauma Behind the Badge – https://www.traumabehindthebadge.us/

Resilient Heroes - https://www.resilient-heroes.com/

COPLINE - https://www.copline.org/   1-800-267-5463

National Suicide & Crisis Lifeline- https://1sthelp.org/ -988

About the Author

Christopher Workman is a career police officer with over 23 years of experience in law enforcement and 30 years as a first responder. He became passionate about mental health and well-being, particularly within the law enforcement community, and has dedicated his time to advocating for the mental health and well-being of officers and providing support and resources to those in need.

He holds an Associate's Degree in Criminal Justice, a Bachelor's Degree in Behavioral Science with a certificate in Emotional Intelligence and Leadership, and is a strong advocate for open dialogue about mental health and believes in the importance of breaking the stigma surrounding seeking help and bringing those issues to the forefront with his podcast, the DeepBlu Project.

Dedicated to the art of learning and networking with first responders across the nation he continues his mission for advancing the profession of law enforcement leadership, promoting networking, enhancing public safety, and advocating for law enforcement and first responder health and mental wellness.

If you are willing to Dive into the Deep End, you will find that you can learn to navigate through the storm.

www.ingramcontent.com/pod-product-compliance
Lightning Source LLC
Chambersburg PA
CBHW031927240526
45464CB00023B/2071